Vimal Ghorecha, Chirag Bhatt

A guide for Selecting Content Management System for Web Application Development

GRIN Publishing

Bibliographic information published by the German National Library:

The German National Library lists this publication in the National Bibliography; detailed bibliographic data are available on the Internet at http://dnb.dnb.de .

Imprint:

Copyright © 2013 GRIN Verlag GmbH
Print and binding: Books on Demand GmbH, Norderstedt Germany
ISBN: 978-3-656-84162-3

This book at GRIN:

http://www.grin.com/en/e-book/283201/a-guide-for-selecting-content-management-system-for-web-application-development

GRIN - Your knowledge has value

Since its foundation in 1998, GRIN has specialized in publishing academic texts by students, college teachers and other academics as e-book and printed book. The website www.grin.com is an ideal platform for presenting term papers, final papers, scientific essays, dissertations and specialist books.

Visit us on the internet:

http://www.grin.com/

http://www.facebook.com/grincom

http://www.twitter.com/grin_com

Research Paper

A guide for Selecting Content Management System for Web Application Development

Vimal Ghorecha[1]
Assistant Professor
Department of MCA
ATMIYA Institute of Technology & Science (AITS)
Gujarat – India

Chirag Bhatt[2]
Assistant Professor
Department of MCA
ATMIYA Institute of Technology & Science (AITS)
Gujarat – India

Abstract: This research paper aims to help for the Website by offering a survey of some methods of PHP comparisons and evaluation studies of Content Management System. This survey shows the good CMS will helpful for users to include different features in the website using plugging and the widget. Here we define the modular architecture and its user interface is modelled (customized) using PHP. We also use the content management system (CMS) to manage the content of the web site by some methods of PHP like Joomla, Wordpress and Drupal. This survey defines the content sector need to undertake more comprehensive and serious studies about the CMS comparisons and evaluation with strength, drawbacks, features etc.

Keywords: CMS, Wordpress, Joomla, Drupal, Web Application Development.

I. Introduction

CMS is used tool to manage website content and depository for information. CMS is a software package that lets you build a website that can be quickly and easily updated by your non-technical staff members. These open source systems are created and supported by a community of developers, and can be downloaded without cost. A web presence is critical for almost every nonprofit, but creating websites can be daunting.

It can take a lot of time, money and technical expertise, which are often in short supply. And just because you have a website up and running doesn't mean your work is done. You still need to keep up with maintenance, updates and desirable new features. This is where an open source Content Management System can help [1].

Content Management Systems (CMS) have evolved into more than just publishing content, but managing your workflow as well. CMS's nowadays allow you to easily conceive, edit, index, and publish content, while giving designers and developers more flexibility in customizing their look and functionality. Although there are many that require advanced skills to operate successfully, this article is going to cover a select few that offer a balance between design, code, and end-user usability [3].

II. Different Content Management System

Content Management Systems are traditionally implemented as document/information 'repositories' of information – generally a content storage location powered by a database technology, with rigorous security controls on the repository to control and audit access to the information stored within. These controls encompass things like:

• User authentication (login);

• Role-based access (check in /check out, edit, make new versions, create/store new content);

• Workflow (initiate, review, approve, comment);

• Auditing [4] [6].

A. Wordpress

Wordpress is web software you can use to create a beautiful website or blog. It started in 2003 with a single bit of code to enhance the typography of everyday writing. Since then it has grown to be the largest self-hosted blogging tool in the world, used on millions of sites and seen by tens of millions of people every day.

Wordpress is a free and open source blogging tool and a content management system (CMS) based on PHP and MySQL. It has many features including a plug-in architecture and a template system. Wordpress is currently the most popular blogging system in use on the Internet. As a free and open source platform, Wordpress relies on peer support. The primary support website is Wordpress.org [7].

B. Drupal

Drupal is a free software package that allows anyone to easily publish, manage and organize a wide variety of content on a website. Hundreds of thousands of people and organizations are using Drupal to power an endless variety of sites.

Drupal you can easily build many different types of web pages - from simple web blogs to large online communities. Drupal design is not as fancy as this of Joomla!, but it is very easy to customize, has built-in search tool and search-engine friendly URL's as an extra module, discussion capabilities and news aggregator. [8].

C. Joomla

Joomla is an award-winning content management system, which enables you to build Web sites and powerful online applications. Many aspects, including its ease-of-use and extensibility, have made Joomla the most popular Web site software available. Best of all, Joomla is an open source solution that is freely available to everyone.

Joomla is one of the best and most widely used CMS applications. It is suitable for creating corporate websites or intranets, online magazines, community-based portals and more. It has numerous built-in features as well as a large selection of extra modules and components which will enhance the value of your website and will enrich your visitors' experience. [8]

Fig. 1 Background of CMS

III. Comparison Based on Features

We collected many features of above three CMSs and compared them. List of features for all three CMS are very large so we include only core features for comparison. In spite of writing features as a point we prepared a feature comparison table which will easily distinguish the features of all three CMS.

Below is The Comparison chart of Wordpress, Joomla and Drupal Based on Features.

Table 1: The Comparison chart of Wordpress, Joomla and Drupal Based on Features [5]

System	Wordpress 3.4|3.5	Joomla 1.5 |1.6	Drupal 6.0|7.0
Ease of Hosting and Installation	●	●	●
Ease of Setup: Simple Site	●	●	●
Ease of Setup: Complex Site	●	●	●
Ease of Use: Content Editors	●	●	●
Ease of Use: Site Administrator	●	●	●
Graphical Flexibility	●	●	●
Accessibility and Search Engine Optimization	●	● | ●	○
Structural Flexibility	●	●	●
User Roles and Workflow	○	○ | ●	●
Community/Web 2.0 Functionality	●	●	●
Extending and Integrating	●	●	●
Security	○	●	●
Support/Community Strength	●	●	●

Fair ○ Solid ● Excellent ●

Table 2: Brief Comparison of Wordpress, Joomla and Drupal

Comparison	Wordpress	Joomla	Drupal
Release Date	5/27/2003	9/16/2005	1/15/2001
Number of Core Versions	3	6	8
Total Number of Updates	105	50	From versions 6.x and 7.x : 39 (including Alpha and Beta)
Number of Plugins/ Modules/Extensions	26,957	7,022	23,246
Number of Themes	1,978	Unknown	1,810
Number of Websites Using The Platform	14.4 %	2.7 %	1.6 %
Popular Sites That Uses Platform	TIME, WSJ.com, NEWSROOM, facebook	IHOP, PORSCHE, E·nopi	MTV, The Economist, the ONION
Most Powerful SEO Extension	Wordpress SEO	AceSEF and sh404SEF	Pathauto
Out-Of-Box SEO Strength	★★★★★	★★★★☆	★★★★☆
India Unique Visits to Main Site	13.4 %	10 %	13.7 %
Ease of Installation			
Ease of Moderation			
Who's It For?			

Vimal Ghorecha [1]
Chirag Bhatt [2]

IV. Conclusion

Today Content management systems (CMS) to help them to deliver targeted information for visitors interested in their products and services, there are many software packages available; however selecting a CMS is sometimes difficult because trend and evaluation data does not always coexist in the same reports.

The results of this report indicate Wordpress, Joomla and Drupal have various strengths and weaknesses. Wordpress is mostly useful for their plug-ins. Joomla provides good basic functionality and is very easy to use, but is missing some key features. Drupal is a good solution for basic and intermediate websites and can be easily administered. Ultimately, the best path for business owners is to use trend data, coupled with their own requirements to choose a CMS that will support their web strategy, both today and in the future.

References

Books:

1. Margaret Rouse, "Content Management System (CMS)" January 2011.
2. CreativeSites, s.r.o.Staré grunty 52, Bratislava, "CONTENT MANAGEMENT SYSTEM (CMS)", 2012
3. Joel Reyes, "How to Evaluate What CMS to Use", Nov 24, 2009
4. Ann Arbour, "Digest of Content Management Systems", October 30, 2006
5. Laura Quinn, Heather Gardner-Madras, "Comparing Open Source Content Management Systems: Wordpress, Joomla, Drupal and Plone", December 2010
6. Absolute North Communications, "Evaluation of Open Source (OS) Content Management Systems (CMS): Alfresco, Drupal, and Joomla!" 18 September 2007

Website:

7. Wikipedia, "Wordpress", http://en.wikipedia.org/wiki/Wordpress, 30 October 2012
8. "Content Management System" http://nmtp05qayyum.Wordpress.com/, 11 February 2011